Basquiat-isms

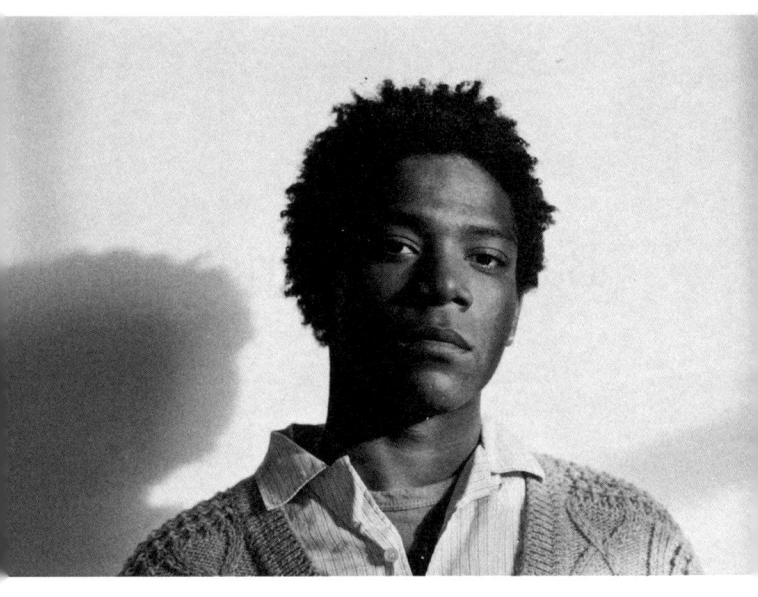

Basquiat-isms

Jean-Michel Basquiat

Edited by Larry Warsh

PRINCETON UNIVERSITY PRESS
Princeton and Oxford

Published by Princeton University Press
41 William Street, Princeton, New Jersey 08540
99 Banbury Road, Oxford OX2 6JX
press.princeton.edu
in association with
No More Rulers
nomorerulers.com
ISMS® is a registered trademark of No More Rulers, Inc.
NO MORE RULERS® is a registered trademark.

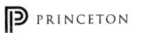

LCCN 2019933105
ISBN 9780691192833
British Library Cataloging-in-Publication Data is available
This book has been composed in Joanna MT
Printed in the China
3 5 7 9 10 8 6 4 2

CONTENTS

INTRODUCTION

Jean-Michel Basquiat endures as a powerful fig-
ure in the art world and beyond, and this book
aims to distill the passion, energy, and spirit
of his extraordinary imagination and bound-
less creativity. Considering the recent history
of twentieth-century global contemporary art,
Basquiat's contribution remains unparalleled
among his peers, and his legacy as a celebrated
artist continues to inspire people around the
world.

This publication was conceived to reveal the
essence of Basquiat's mind through his highly
poetic and distinctive thought processes. The
phrases herein are culled from various sources,
including interviews, articles, and recordings of
the artist in conversation. As an early admirer

and collector of his work, I am humbled by this compilation of Basquiat's ideas that resound with all the passion and intensity of his singular worldview.

Basquiat was born in Brooklyn, New York, in 1960 to parents of Haitian–Puerto Rican descent. During his youth he expressed interest in art, and as a mature teenager he became active in Manhattan's colorful downtown art scene. By his early twenties Basquiat was a revered artist immersed in the thriving culture of the times and rose to fame alongside figures such as Andy Warhol, Keith Haring, Madonna, Debbie Harry, and other well-known eccentrics. Basquiat died an untimely death in 1988 at the youthful age of twenty-seven—at the height of his artistic stardom. Although we still mourn the loss of this creative giant, the raw energy of his contribution continues to reach far and wide.

As Henry Geldzahler once eloquently wrote:

Jean-Michel lived a short life, but he left us with a lot of memorable work, an astonishing amount given the number of his working years. The ancient Greeks believed that lives were not tragically short or satisfyingly long; rather, they thought, each life is lived to its own termination, and should be valued in its own terms. One might think of him as a warrior who fell too soon in a battle not of his making.

Almost every work Basquiat produced contained some form of written word. As art critic René Ricard wrote in an unpublished essay, "Had he reached artistic maturity at a slightly earlier (or later) time, Jean-Michel Basquiat would have manifested as a poet." Even Basquiat himself once stated: "I'm going to become a writer. I want to become a writer. But I can't write."[1] Indeed, writing was always central to Basquiat's artistic practice. From his early collaborative work as SAMO©, a text-based take on graffiti he produced on the streets of New York City from the late seventies through the early eighties, to his ongoing studio practice where text was integral to his visual vocabulary, the shards of language, often elusive in exact meaning and posed in the savvy staccato of urban vernacular, come together as a patchwork quilt of offhand provocations throughout his oeuvre into an extended, improvisatory kind of epic poem. Typically scrawled across his artwork in his characteristic all-capital letters, be it as enigmatic asides or titular titles, Basquiat's texts within his canvases are as much a part of what he told us as the sum of those few interviews he granted in his lifetime, with punchy phrases like:

"FAMOUS NEGRO ATHLETES"

"PLUSH SAFE HE THINK"

"MOST YOUNG KINGS GET THEIR HEAD CUT OFF"

"JIMMY BEST ON HIS BACK TO THE
SUCKERPUNCH OF HIS CHILDHOOD FILES"

"LOVE IS A LIE
LOVER = LIAR"

"ALOT OF BOWERY BUMS USED TO BE
EXECUTIVES"

"BOOM FOR REAL"

"ROME PAYS OFF ©"

"IT ALL DEPENDS WHO YOU ARE ON WHAT
STREET"

"VOICES OF AUTHORITY MAKE MAJOR CLAIMS"

"HOLLYWOOD AFRICANS IN FRONT OF THE
CHINESE THEATER WITH FOOTPRINTS OF
MOVIESTARS"

Though he never collected all the language that ran rampant through his mind like unruly youth in a schoolyard into anything as formal as a book—he always made the words subservient to the images in his art, and was, for someone so smart, articulate, and knowledgeable, notably reticent about speaking in public or for the record—Basquiat *was* a writer. Many years ago, I was blessed with the opportunity to collect Basquiat's series of handwritten journals known as "The Notebooks" (published in facsimile form by Princeton University Press). The notebooks are distinct works of art in themselves, filled with highly poetic words and phrases, such as those above, laid out in a deliberately visual manner. It was through the study of these notebooks that I was inspired to explore another side of his voice—his spoken words—which evolved into this publication. Condensed from the limited yet rich supply of firsthand material that exists, this book aims to give a more direct sense of who Basquiat was, how he spoke, and how he expressed himself in words.

The book is comprised of four chapters: "Process," "Influence and Heroes," "New York," and "Art." "Process" explores the motivations, ideas, and techniques behind Basquiat's art practice. "Influence and Heroes" reveals his source material and the forces that shaped him as an artist. "New York" chronicles his experience of the city, both as a young child growing up in Brooklyn and as an initially struggling artist who quickly achieved art world fame. The final chapter, "Art," delves into Basquiat's unique perspectives, opinions, and experiences of art, the art world, and what it means to be an artist.

Basquiat was not ahead of his time; he was his time. He was an artist, a poet, a critical thinker, a celebrity, a musician, an actor, and a wild child of the universe, full of consistencies and inconsistencies, whose artistic courage and bravery defined an era. It is my hope that this book provides a glimpse into Basquiat's incredible mind through his less examined spoken words, and serves as a foundation of thought for generations to come. May his words and thoughts enliven your thinking today as much as they have inspired me for many decades.

LARRY WARSH

Basquiat-isms

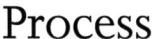

Process

The more I paint, the more I like everything.
(1)

———

Believe it or not, I can actually draw. (2)

———

I start with a picture and then finish it.
I don't think about art while I work.
I try to think about life. (3)

———

I like the [paintings] where I don't paint
as much as others, where it's just a
direct idea. (1)

———

Magic doesn't especially interest me. What I
like is the intuition that tells me that a work is
finished. I'm not an elitist but an autodidact
who would like to be part of the family
of artists. (4)

———

You think there's frustration in your art?

No, no. But I think frustration caused me
to do a lot of it. (5)

———

I usually put a lot down and then I take a lot away, then I put some more down and then I take some more away, so it's like a constant editing process. (5)

———

I cross out words to move them into the background. (3)

———

I cross out words so you will see them more; the fact that they are obscured makes you want to read them. (6)

———

Sometimes I just want to retract [words, so
I cross them out]. They might stick out a little
bit too much, the words. So the line kind
of blends [them] into the rest of
the painting. (5)

———

[I like] words that jump off the page when
I see them. (7)

———

I look at the words I like and copy them over
and over again, or use diagrams. (7)

———

[The lists were] from going to Italy and copying names out of tour books and condensed histories. (1)

———

It's pretty primal, whatever I feel at the moment? Sometimes it's political, I don't know. (8)

———

I want to make paintings that look as if they were made by a child. (9)

I like kids' work more than work by real
artists any day. (10)

———

I don't know how to describe my work,
because it's not always the same thing. It's like
asking somebody, asking Miles [Davis], "How
does your horn sound?" I don't think he
could really tell you why he plays this at
this point in the music. You're sort of
on automatic. (11)

———

[With] music, you have to work with other people, and I don't work with other people to do my painting. I don't collaborate with other people. (7)

———

I trained myself, you know. (7)

———

I've discovered that I think I rather work alone, more than anything. I used to have assistants, a lot, around me. And then on days when they wouldn't come, I would be a lot more productive. (11)

———

I was working under my own steam. (3)

———

I was trying to communicate an idea;
I was trying to paint a very urban landscape.
I was trying to make paintings different from
the paintings that I saw a lot of at the time,
which were mostly minimal, and they were
highbrow and alienating, and I wanted to
make very direct paintings that most
people would feel the emotion behind
when they saw them. (7)

———

Do you think you are lucky?

Talented, too. (12)

———

I don't wanna be too wordy. I want people
to understand me; I don't want to mumble
too much or anything like that. (7)

———

I am, what I am, what I am. (5)

———

I like the copyrights because they look good. (3)

———

I feel if I work randomly, I come up with a more interesting narrative. (5)

———

Do you work best late at night or do you have a certain time that's ... ?

Anytime is good; there's not one time better than the other. (11)

———

Do you feel like a victim?

Yes. (3)

———

I think that appearance is really a lot. (7)

———

I like to have information rather than just have
a brushstroke. Just to have these words to put
in these feelings underneath. (7)

———

[My art] is usually how I feel at the moment.
(7)

[I get work done because] I just don't know
what else to do with myself. (1)

The first paintings I made were on windows
I found on the street. And I used the
window shape as a frame and I just put
the painting on the glass part and on
doors I found on the street. (11)

I did some drawings when I was fifteen, sixteen, seventeen that were just junk teenage stuff … ; then when I was nineteen and things got more realistic for me in my life … the work also became more realistic. (7)

———

[The transition to canvas] just sort of happened. I did more drawings up to a certain point. (5)

———

[I work from] sketches, gluing paper down onto canvases. It usually has to do with that day. (5)

———

I use a lot of canvas, but I've become bored with it now, and I just want to use wood for everything, as the base for the paintings. I think it looks much better, less academic. I enjoy painting on canvas still, sometimes, but I really prefer wood and working with more odd shapes. In the beginning I worked on wood because that's always free, to work on the doors and windows of the Lower East Side. And then I started working on canvas when I got into a gallery. No, cut that. I started to work on canvas before that. I like some of the canvases I've done, but I really enjoy the wood more. (7)

———

Everything is well stretched even though it looks like it may not be. (1)

Lately I've been taking all these paintings that are older. And some that I thought were less successful and cropping them. To four foot, four by three squares. And then hinging them in to these long kind of comic strip–looking things. (5)

For a while I was drawing on good paper,
but now I've gone back to the bad stuff.
I put matte medium on it. If you put matte
medium on it, it seals it up, so it doesn't
really matter. (1)

———

I don't think there's anything under that gold
paint. Most of the paintings have one or two
paintings under them. I'm worried that in the
future, parts might fall off and some of the
heads underneath might show through. (1)

———

A lot of [the figures in my paintings] are self-portraits and some of them are just my friends. (7)

———

I don't have that many political thoughts in my work. Most of my thoughts are just pretty personal. Happiness, just very simple thoughts. (7)

———

I wanted to put a metal Roman belt buckle on this painting. I went over to the Metropolitan Museum and I did the drawing of the buckle, and then I came back with it and I put it right [on the painting]. (5)

———

I think I have to learn more not to work around what's around me and just work with what I think. I shouldn't let what's around me affect my work at all. I should just work on what I normally work on. (11)

———

I was making [a drawing] in an airplane
once. I was copying some stuff out of a
Roman sculpture book. This lady said,
"Oh, what are you studying?" I said,
"It's a drawing." (1)

———

Originally I wanted to copy the whole history
down, but it was too tedious so I just stuck to
the cast of characters. (1)

———

I usually take paper with me when I go away,
try to do as much of that as I can. (11)

———

I take suggestions, too. I work with some people. Something might be bothering me and I'll just ask somebody. (5)

———

I'm not out to frighten people. (7)

———

You start working on illustration board and stuff when you're at school, and you erase all the time. You know what I mean? (5)

———

I don't know how much the market influences
me, really. [I choose my colors] by what's left.
I usually get the same colors every time.
Naphthol Crimson, Vulcan Blue. I cut them
with white sometimes. Sometimes out of
the drawing. (5)

———

Is there any logic [in the juxtapositions]?
God, man. If you're talking to Marcel
Duchamp, you ask him, or even Rauschenberg
or something. You couldn't tell them why
something is next to something else,
except for that it's just there. (5)

———

Every once in a while [I do self-portraits]. (1)

———

Occasionally, when I get mad at a woman,
I'll do some great, awful painting about her.
Sometimes [she knows]. Sometimes not.
Sometimes I don't even know it. It's just those
little mental icons of the time. (1)

———

I produce records; I did one rap record. Now I
am working on an African drum album. (12)

———

I think [alchemy] worked. Because I was
writing gold on all this stuff, and I made
all this money right afterward. (1)

———

I had some money. I made the best paintings
ever. I was completely reclusive. (10)

———

Now I lead a pretty solitary life, you know. (13)

———

So do you want to live?

Of course I want to live. (1)

———

I think my mind affects my work more now
than it used to; I used to work more heart to
hand ... I think that as you get older, you can't
help it; the mind just pulls into it. (7)

———

People think I'm burning out, but I'm not.
Some days I can't get an idea, and I think,
man, I'm just washed up, but it's
just a mood. (10)

———

I think I'm more economical now. Every line
means something. (10)

———

Influence and Heroes

If you wanna talk about influence, man, then you've got to realize that influence is not influence. It's simply someone's idea going through my new mind. (14)

———

Anything can act as an influence. If I see a painting from the Middle Ages, I can see the life, I can see how people were. Like seeing a sculpture from Africa, I can see the tribe, I can see the life around it. (7)

———

I get my facts from books, stuff on atomizers,
the blues, ethyl alcohol, geese in Egyptian
glyphs. I don't take credit for my facts. The
facts exist without me. (15)

———

[I have nostalgia] for everything. But just
the objects, not the people of periods, just
the objects. (12)

———

I'm usually in front of the television. I have
to have some source material around me
to work off. (11)

———

[The words come from] real life, books, television. When I'm working I hear them, you know. I just throw them down. (5)

———

Leonardo [da Vinci] kept a lot of his own records. (16)

———

When I was younger I looked at pop art. Dada was the thing I looked most at. Mostly in books and museums. (7)

[My earliest memory is] getting hit by a car. I was playing in the street; I was seven or eight years old. It seemed very dreamlike. It was just like in the movies, where they slow it down. When a car's coming at you, it was just like that. I had an operation in my stomach, the whole business. I remember it just being very dreamlike, and seeing the car coming at me and then just seeing everything through sort of a red filter. (11)

———

I grew up in a principle American background. (5)

———

I thought I wanted to be a cartoonist when I was younger, and then I changed to painting when I was about fifteen or so. (11)

———

I was just pretty naive as a kid, mostly. I never thought about professions or anything. That's what I mean by "naive." I never thought about what I'd be doing to make money, stuff like that, I never thought about it. (11)

———

I've never been to Africa. I'm an artist who
has been influenced by his New York
environment. But I have a cultural memory.
I don't need to look for it, it exists. It's over
there, in Africa That doesn't mean that
I have to go live here. Our cultural
memory follows us everywhere,
wherever you live. (4)

———

Probably Robert Farris Thompson I thought
wrote the best thing—the guy that wrote
Flash of the Spirit, which is probably the
best book I ever read on African art.
It's one of the best. (11)

———

I wouldn't say a lot [about art history], but that's the majority of the time the kinds of books I read. (5)

———

I went out and bought some books that were about anatomy. [I'm] not really imitating [them]. I use them as a source material. (5)

———

I like Mark Twain books a lot. (11)

———

I was going to say Burroughs, but I thought I'd sound too young. Because everybody [says] Burroughs all the time. But he's my favorite living author. Definitely. I think it's really close to what Mark Twain writes, as far as the point of view. (11)

———

I have a couple Warhols and I have a Picasso. A 1922 oil painting. I took all my money and I bought that so I wouldn't spend it all. (11)

———

[James Van Der Zee] was really great. He [had] a great sense of the "good" picture. (1)

I just wanted to meet [Andy Warhol]; he was an art hero of mine. (10)

———

[Leonardo da Vinci] is my favorite artist. (5)

———

There weren't that many painters [around me]. There were a few. There were mostly punk rocker musicians and the New Wave filmmakers. (7)

———

People expect you not to really change;
they want you to be the same as you were
when you were nineteen. (7)

———

Bebop's I guess my favorite music. But I don't
listen to it all the time; I listen to
everything. (11)

———

I think about all my heroes, Charlie Parker,
Jimi Hendrix. I had a romantic feeling of how
people had become famous. Even when
I didn't think my stuff was that good,
I'd have faith. (10)

———

[Andy Warhol and I] worked for a year on about a million paintings. (11)

———

With me and Andy [Warhol], we worked in the same place on the same paintings, instead of moving the paintings from studio to studio as we did with Clemente. (11)

———

[Andy Warhol] would start most of the paintings. He would put something very concrete or recognizable, like a newspaper headline or a product logo, and then I would sort of deface it, and then I would try to get him to work some more on it, and then I would work more on it. I would try to get him to do at least two things, you k now? He likes to do just one hit and then have me do all the work after that. (11)

———

The black person is the protagonist in most
of my paintings. I realized that I didn't
see many paintings with black
people in them. (10)

———

**Black people in this country get a rough deal.
Is that part of what your work's about?**

Yeah, I have to say so. (7)

———

Of course there is [anger in me],
of course there is.

What are you angry about?

I don't remember. (7)

———

[My work is] about 80 percent anger.

But there's also humor.

People laugh when you fall on your ass.
What's humor? (1)

———

Probably seeing [Picasso's] *Guernica* was my
favorite thing when I was a kid. (11)

———

I liked Rauschenberg a lot when I used to live
on the Lower East Side. (11)

———

I was just taking a bad example from the wrong people, is what happened. (11)

———

The country makes me more paranoid. I think the crazy people out there are a little crazier. (1)

———

[When you see an old painting], even with things that aren't so obvious, like the abstract expressionist painters and so on and so forth, it looks like New York in the '50s. They seem to be true historical documents. I can get more from them than reading or other things. (7)

———

Listening to what [Andy Warhol] had to say was probably the most fun. Seeing how he dealt with things was probably the best part. Because he's really funny. Tells a lot of funny jokes. (11)

———

[Andy Warhol's influence on me?] I wear clean pants all the time now. (10)

[The artists I like best are] Twombly, Rauschenberg, Warhol, John, Da Vinci's and Titian's drawings. More recently work by Penck, Clemente, Cucchi. (4)

My favorite Twombly is *Apollo and the Artist*, with the big Apollo written across it. (1)

[The Warhol collaboration] was very simple.
I just had to push him, because he's a bit lazy.
He hadn't drawn for twenty years. (3)

———

I was the one who helped Andy Warhol paint!
It had been twenty years since he'd touched
a brush. Thanks to our collaboration, he was
able to rediscover his relationship
to painting. (4)

———

Because of people like Andy [Warhol], I think
that the artist can be viewed more as a hero,
an image. (7)

———

[I'm a hero] the way an actor can be a hero,
the way a musician can be a hero. (7)

———

[My subject matter is] royalty, heroism,
and the streets. (1)

———

New York

Since I was seventeen, I thought I might be a star. (17)

———

This city is crawling with uptight, middle-class pseudos trying to look like the money they don't have. Status symbols. It cracks me up. It's like they're walking around with price tags stapled to their heads. People should live more spiritually, man. But we can't stand on the sidewalk all day screaming at people to clean up their acts, so we write on walls. (18)

———

You just end up surviving when you have to.
(11)

I tried to paint like the Lower East Side and what it was like to live there. Spanish things from the neighborhood like bodegas, images, and stuff like that. (7)

I came from a brownstone house with a backyard, pretty quiet. My father worked hard; my mother stayed at home and looked after us. (7)

My whole life I went to school and I came home, and that was it. I really didn't have any friends or anything. I just kind of stayed home and went to school, over and over again.
I went to the movies once in a while.
I always enjoyed drawing. (5)

———

Usually the other kids who didn't have friends, I'd be friends with. (11)

———

I was a cute kid. (9)

———

I did well in English and History. I just didn't participate in school at all. I'd just be drawing at my desk. (11)

———

I went to high school for a little while, where I made those typical teenage psychedelic pictures of people's faces with stars. I was also selling handmade postcards, and hand-painted abstract expressionist sweatshirts, to make money. (19)

———

Jean-Michel discussing the possibility of throwing a pie at their principal during graduation

It became a dare. This girl said, "Are you really going to do it? It would be great." I bought some whipped cream and tried to fill a box, but it didn't work. Then I tried a can of shaving cream. He was wearing a white jacket so it looked like a magic trick. When the box fell off there was no reaction from the audience. They were supposed to applaud the speech, but they didn't want to do that, and they didn't want to laugh either. There didn't seem to be much point in going back [to school]. (20)

———

I was just mostly being weird. (11)

———

I don't think I dealt with reality that
much really. (11)

———

I went [to the Mudd Club] every night for
two years. At that time I had no apartment,
so I just used to go there to see what my
prospects were. (1)

———

Aesthetically I really hated Club 57. I thought it was silly. All this old and bad shit. I'd rather see something old and good. (20)

———

My graffiti was separate from all the graffiti. I didn't hang out with people. I didn't go to the yards. I didn't hoard cans of spray paint. (5)

———

I hung to myself a lot. (19)

———

The problem of money became imperative.
I couldn't even buy the necessary materials to
finish a canvas. I thought about going to see
the Art Students League. I had enough
curiosity, enough will to find a solution,
a way of reaching any goal. (4)

———

I tried to get into Parsons because a couple
of years earlier I had no money. Somebody
told me that if you went to art school that
they would pay your outside life too.
So I looked into this. But it never really
happened. And I'm kind of grateful. (5)

———

I wanted to build up a name for myself. (1)

———

I think the Brooklyn [Museum] is my favorite,
but I never go much. (1)

———

[They spend millions of taxpayers' dollars
each year cleaning up graffiti but] that's a
drop in the bucket compared to how people
are getting shafted in big ways. (18)

———

I try to be a little reclusive, and not just to be out there and be brought up and brought down, like they do with most of them. (7)

———

Most of my reviews have been more reviews of my personality ... More so than my work. (11)

———

They knew more about my graffiti and stuff like that, and as more of a personality than as a painter, when I was younger. (7)

———

I can't get taxis. I go on the street, wave my
hand, and they just drive past me. Normally
I have to wait for three or four cabs. A few taxi
companies tell their drivers not to pick
up blacks. Black taxi drivers drive
past me, too. (3)

———

[Not seeing so much black art in Western
society] could be something as simple as the
racism of the gallery owner, or the racism of
the museum directors. I mean that. (7)

———

What she really wanted were my paintings. She tried to tell me that her chauffeur, who was black, worked with her in her gallery, not that he was her driver. (10)

I did some postcards with John Sex. He had a really great mind. [And Kenny Scharf], I knew he was going to be famous the minute I met him. (20)

I just wanted to do a record. I was in some bands for a while. I played this club circuit thing. Actually, before I started painting a lot I was kind of in this band. It was called Gray. (5)

[Gray] was a noise band. I played a guitar with a file, and a synthesizer. I was inspired by John Cage at the time—music that isn't really music. We were trying to be incomplete, abrasive, oddly beautiful. (10)

Didn't you pick up Debbie Harry at one point and take her to a loft?

Well, she was a bag lady and I kissed her and she turned into a fairy princess. (11)

[Annina Nosei's] was the first time I had a place to work. I took it. Not seeing the drawbacks until later. She used to bring collectors down there, so it wasn't very private. I didn't mind. I was young. (9)

———

[Annina Nosei] offered me her cellar to work in. The bad thing about this situation was that she sold paintings that weren't finished. She said someone was interested in the painting and sold it despite my protests. I was young then. I've learned a lot since then.

(3)

———

They set it up for me so I'd have to make eight
paintings in a week, for the show the next
week. That was one of the things I didn't like.
I made them in this big warehouse there.
Annina, Mazzoli, and Bruno were there.
It was like a factory, a sick factory.
I hated it. (10)

———

Diego gave me my first show—Diego Cortez.
(11)

———

I went to Interview magazine and bugged Andy
Warhol, you know, to find out how to get
closer to it. Then I was in Diego Cortez's *New
York/New Wave* show at P.S. 1. In those days
I never had enough money to cover a whole
canvas. I wouldn't be surprised if I died
like a boxer, really broke, but somehow
I doubt it. (19)

———

One day [Julian Schnabel] came into Annina
[Nosei]'s gallery. And I asked him if he wanted
to spar. I figured even if I lost, I couldn't
look bad. (1)

———

They have this image of me: wild man running—you know, wild monkey man, whatever the fuck they think. (11)

———

I get all these telegrams. It's fun. You never know what it could be. "You're drafted." "I have $2,000 for you." It could be anything. And because people are spending more money with telegrams, they get right to the point. But now my bell rings at all hours of the night. I pretend I'm not home. (1)

———

I haven't decided what part of the world isn't going to get blown up so I don't know where to put [a house]. (1)

———

Yes, [people] always do [turn on you]. I can't think of one big celebrity-type person they haven't done that to.

Have they done that to you?

Here and there. (7)
They still call me a graffiti artist. They don't call Keith or Kenny graffiti artists anymore. (9)

———

I got taken advantage of. (11)

———

**Your work does reflect an interest in all kinds
of intellectual areas that go beyond the streets, and it's
the combination of the two.**

It's more of a name-dropping thing. (1)

———

I think I have to give [the street art] crown
to Keith Haring. I haven't worked in the streets
in so long. (1)

———

I hardly ever [go out] now. I mean sometimes. But really not as much as the old days. It's not the way it was then, anymore. (11)

———

I can't relate so much to the kids that go out these days. All these young, perfect kids. It's not the same sort of artistic climate as it was back then. (9)

———

[I try] seeing as little as possible of all these art people around me. [But when I leave New York] I get bored everywhere else. (3)

———

You know, I wasn't [bad]; I wasn't a
troublemaker, I just didn't really participate
much in school. (11)

———

I enjoy that they think I'm a bad boy.
I think it's great. (11)

———

Art

The greatest treasures of the world are art. They are the most lasting; they are still here after people. (7)

———

I don't listen to what art critics say. I don't know anybody who needs a critic to find out what art is. (3)

———

People have a very short attention span. They're looking for another artist every six months or year. And it's really impossible. There's only twenty good artists in a century. (13)

———

At that point, [an artist] was somebody who could draw, but my ideas have changed since then. Now I see an artist as something a lot broader than that. (15)

———

Rap music and graffiti? Those both have evolved into fashions more than actual cultural expressions. See, a lot of people that do graffiti went to art and design high schools. See what I mean? (5)

———

If an artist is really good, you wouldn't be teaching him. (5)

I never learned anything about art in school. (16)

I wanted to be an artist ever since I was three years old. (3)

I didn't paint 'til I was twelve years old. (7)

———

I was a really lousy artist as a kid. Too abstract
expressionist; or I'd draw a big ram's head,
really messy. I'd never win painting contests.
I remember losing to a guy who did
a perfect Spider-Man. (1)

———

I really wanted to be the best artist in the
class, but my work had a really ugly edge to it.
(1)

———

I don't know if my being black has anything to do with my success. I don't think I should be compared to black artists but with all artists. (3)

———

There's really nothing else to do in life, except flirt with girls. If I'm away from painting for a week, I get bored. (10)

———

The art was mostly minimal when I came up, and it sort of confused me a little bit. I thought it divided people a little bit. I thought it alienated most people from art. (11)

———

I was more interested in attacking the gallery circuit ... I didn't think about doing painting. I was thinking about making fun of the paintings that were in there, more than making paintings. (11)

———

I really don't think the art world exists. I really don't think it exists. I mean, there's people who like paintings and then there's dealers and then there's people who work at the museum, but I don't think they're collectively an "art world." There's a few good artists and then everything else is extra. (11)

———

I think I like seeing [paintings] in museums
more than anything else, but I've seen them in
all those different places; I don't object to
seeing them there, it's just part of it.
[I feel that I am part of a tradition, that
I am moving along in a line]. I think
art is very important. (7)

———

Labels don't mean anything. My work has
nothing to do with graffiti. It's painting, it
always has been. I've always painted. Well
before painting was in fashion. (4)

———

The thing is that graffiti has a lot of rules in it as to what you can do and what you can't do, and I think it's hard to make art under those conditions. It has to include your name and … it has to have a certain, I don't know. (11)

———

James Rosenquist told me that art isn't show business, and I think that's something that I have to remember. It's a bad frame of mind for the artist in a way, because it makes you too regular, and you don't want to be. I want clarity but I also want to have some sort of obscurity. I want [the work] to be more cryptic. (7)

———

I'd say my mother gave me all the primary things. The art came from her. (21)

I remember my mother drawing stuff out of the Bible. Like Samson knocking down, breaking the temple down, stuff like this. (11)

[My first reaction to selling work was] overconfidence, I guess. Super confidence. I was just happy that I was able to stick it out and then get things I wanted. I just felt really right. I felt like I was glad that I stuck it out, and I was glad that I'd had these hard times. (11)

———

[My first show in Modena] was fun because it was the first time, but financially it was pretty stupid. (1)

———

[When I show in Europe], usually I just
have to go myself and I have to pay my own
ticket because I don't know how to ask
diplomatically. And then I usually want
to go with friends so I have to pay for
them as well. (1)

———

People are getting credit now for graffiti as if
it were something new, but they're really fifth
or tenth string. (19)

———

[The art press is] not one person. They just
rely on third- and fourth-hand information
too much. I'm more reluctant to talk to them
for fear of putting my foot in my own mouth.
I mean, they misquote, quote me out
of context. (5)

———

They talk about graffiti endlessly; I don't really
consider myself to be a graffiti artist. (11)

———

[If I didn't paint, I'd be] directing movies, I guess. Ones in which black people are portrayed as being people of the human race. And not aliens and not all negative and not all thieves and drug dealers and the whole bit. Just real stories. (11)

———

I'm doing an interview but I'm saying too much. (20)

———

I don't think it's good to be honest in interviews; I think it's better to lie. (11)

———

If I tell the truth I'm going to sound like an egomaniac. (20)

———

Do you feel like talking about your paintings?

Let's just talk and get it over with. (18)

———

I hate to talk about painting. (11)

———

I don't want to give a one-word answer is
what it is. (11)

What would you do if the artist you were
writing about were dead? Do it like that.
Pretend I'm dead. (3)

I think [J. Edgar Hoover] is interesting. [He]
would make the great American novel. I wrote
to [him] as a kid. I sent him a drawing.
I didn't get any letter back. It was one of
the first art things I did. I must have been
eight or nine. It was a design
for a gun. (16)

I was joking one day and thought, maybe I should go to the Art Students League—to see if it's really conducive to anything—but students' work is so sad. (19)

———

I know so little about my career, to tell you the truth. I don't know who has what or anything like that really, or even what they paid for it most of the time. (11)

———

All my friends sold the paintings I gave them. Pretty much all of them. (13)

———

You like to be called the "Black Picasso"?

Not so much. It's flattering, but I think it's also demeaning. (12)

———

I think black people are glad to be represented and recognized in my paintings, and that's the feeling I get when we talk about it. (7)

———

I prefer the more offhand statements [about my work] more than the ones coming from qualified sources. (7)

I can't say that I'm the first recognized black artist, because there's a lot of people, Jacob Lawrence and a lot of other people. Maybe I'm the first to get across to a lot of people. (7)

———

Aren't you worried that you might run out of ideas and people won't be interested in you anymore?

Sure. There's nothing I can do about it. (14)

———

I think there's a lot of people that are neglected in art. I don't know if it's because of who made the paintings or what, but black people are never really portrayed realistically in—not even portrayed in—modern art enough, and I'm glad that I do that. I use "black" as the protagonist because I am black, and that's why I use it as the main character in all the paintings. (7)

———

I had more artist friends before I began
to make money; now only other artists who
make money want to see me. I feel much
happier now—my whole life is focused.
Before there was all this energy, and
nowhere to put it. (19)

———

I'm not really sure if the stories of the artists
in the studio quietly working are really true
anymore. There's always photographers
coming to the studio, and stuff like that.
It's a life that is documented and put out
there. You go to a restaurant and they write
about it in the *Post* on page six. (7)

———

[I use the black character in the same way as Matisse used the white character]. Just for a change. I don't think bad of Matisse at all; his paintings are beautiful. That's what was around him. (7)

―――――

Am I surprised [at my success]? I used to be more surprised. (5)

―――――

Usually I have to check up on these dealers and make sure they're showing the right work. Or just make sure that it's right. (1)

―――――

My dealers [have the largest number of my paintings]. Probably Bruno [Bischofberger].
(11)

[Girlfriends, dealers,] they're about the same, actually. (1)

When they were making Dada, when Picasso was around, [the critics said] the same stuff about art being dead. Those guys are outside of art, you know what I mean? Too [many] free dinners. They drink cheap wine at the openings, they get drunk, and they get nasty.
(12)

The most identifiable things are what
[the dealers] like. I did some portraits last year
and they really hated those. But the artists
like them. (11)

———

I think it's good that people are more
respectful to artists, instead of seeing them
as junk oddballs or whatever they saw
them as before. (7)

———

I wanted to be a star, not a gallery mascot. (10)

———

I think I make [art] for myself, but ultimately I
think I make it for the world. (7)

———

Making good art is revenge enough. That's why I feel no nostalgia for the misery I lived in. All my energy scattered then, without following any particular path. Now I'm a lot happier. (4)

———

I never went to art school. I failed the art courses that I did take in school. I just looked at a lot of things. And that's how I learnt about art, by looking at it. (21)

———

I don't like to discuss art at all. (12)

———

SOURCES

1. Basquiat, Jean-Michel. "From the Subways to SoHo." Interview by Henry Geldzahler. *Interview* magazine, no. 13, January 1983. https://www.interviewmagazine.com/art /jean-michel-basquiat-henry-geldzahler.

2. Hoffman, Fred, with Acquavella Galleries. *Jean-Michel Basquiat Drawing: Work from the Schorr Family Collection.* New York: Rizzoli, 2014, 12–13.

3. Basquiat, Jean-Michel. "Waiting for Basquiat." Interview by Isabella Graw. *Wolkenkratzer Art Journal*, Frankfurt, no. 1, January–February 1987.

4. Basquiat, Jean-Michel. Interview by Demosthenes Davvetas. *New Art International*, no. 3, October–November 1988, 10–15. Reprinted in *Jean-Michel Basquiat*, edited by Lucas Marenzi. Milan: Charter 1999, lxii–lxiii.

5. Tschinkel, Paul (producer). *Jean-Michel Basquiat: An Interview.* Filmed interview with Marc H. Miller, 1989 (no. 30a in the video series ART/New York). VHS, 34 minutes. Distributed by Inner Tube Films, New York. Transcribed by Anke Weidmann.

6. *Jean-Michel Basquiat.* Exhibition catalog. Lugano, Switzerland: Museo d'Arte Moderna Cittá di Lugano, 2005, 87. https://www.guggenheim-bilbao.eus/en/guia-educadores/experimental-techniques/.

7. Dunlop, Geoff, and Sandy Nairne. "Andy Warhol and Jean-Michel Basquiat." Channel 4 with WDR Koln, 11 January–15 February 1987, *State of the Art*, episode 6. https://www.youtube.com/watch?time_continue=131&v=foerFJqupYM. Reprinted in *Basquiat: Boom for Real*, 262–67 (see source 15).

8. Basquiat, Jean-Michel. Interview by Glenn O'Brien on *TV Party*, 1979. https://vk.com/video-930575_151940093.

9. Haden-Guest, Anthony. "Burning Out." *Vanity Fair*, November 1988.

10. McGuigan, Cathleen. "New Art, New Money: The Marketing of an American Artist." *New York Times*, February 10, 1985. https://archive.nytimes.com/www.nytimes.com/books/98/08/09/specials/basquiat-mag.html?platform=hootsuite.

11. Basquiat, Jean-Michel. "I Have to Have Some Source Material around Me." Interview by Becky Johnston and Tamra Davis, Beverly Hills, California, 1985. Reprinted in *Basquiat*, edited by Dieter Buchhart and Sam Kelle. Exhibition catalog. Fondation Beyeler (May 9–September 5, 2010) and Musée d'Art Moderne de la Ville de Paris (October 15, 2010–January 30, 2011), Ostfildern, Hatje Kantz 2010, xxi–xxx.

12. Basquiat, Jean-Michel. "The House of Jean-Michel Basquiat." Interview by Lisa Licitra Ponti. *Domus* magazine, no. 646, Editoriale Domus SpA, Rozzano, Milano, January 1984, 66–68.

13. Haden-Guest, Anthony. *True Colors: The Real Life of the Art World.* New York: Atlantic Monthly Press, 1996.

14. Artnet. http://www.artnet.com/artists/jean-michel -basquiat/past-auction-results/31.

15. Buchhart, Dieter, and Eleanor Nairne, with Lotte Johnson, eds. *Basquiat: Boom for Real.* Munich: Prestel in collaboration with Barbicon Center, 2017, 189.

16. De Antonio, Emilio. "Art: Radical Views on 'Painters Painting.'" Interview with Jean-Michel Basquiat. *Interview* magazine, July 1984, 49–50.

17. Buchhart, Dieter, and Tricia Laughlin Bloom, eds. *Basquiat: The Unknown Notebooks.* New York: Skira Rizzoli Publications in collaboration with the Brooklyn Museum, 2015, 24.

18. Faflick, Philip. "SAMO© Graffiti: BOOSH-WAH or CIA?" *Village Voice,* December 11, 1978.

19. Gablik, Suzi. "Report from New York: The Graffiti Question." *Art in America,* 70, October 1982, 33–39.

20. Hager, Steven. "The Mudd Club." In *Art after Midnight.* New York: St. Martin's Press, 1986, 38–115.

21. Manatakis, Lexi. "Jean-Michel Basquiat in His Own Words." *Dazed Digital,* November 21, 2017. http://www.dazeddigital.com/art-photography/article /38129/1/-jean-michel-basquiat-in-his-own-words.

JEAN MICHEL BASQUIAT BORN DEC. 22/1960/BROOKLYN/N.Y.)

MOTHER: PUERTO RICAN (FIRST GENERATION)
FATHER: HA PORT·AU PRINCE, HAITI.

ST. ANNS
?
(DIVORCED)
[NAME OF THE TOWN]

P.S. 6
P.S. 101
P.S. 45 ← (SOME CATHOLIC SCHOOL
I.S. 293   DURING YEAR + ½ IN
CITY AS SCHOOL   PUERTO RICO

11 TH GRADE DROPOUT

ⓑ PUT A BOX OF SHAVING
CREAM IN PRINCIPAL'S
FACE AT GRADUATION

FIRST AMBITION: FIREMAN
FIRST ARTISTIC AMBITION: CARTOONIST.

NO POINT
IN GOOF
IN GOING
BACK

EARLY THEMES WERE THE:

①. THE SEAVIEW FROM "VOYAGE TO THE BOTTOM OF THE SEA"
2. ALFRED. E. NEUMAN
3. ALFRED HITHCOCK (HIS FACE OVER + OVER)
4. NIXON
5. CARS (MOSTLY DRAGSTER)S.
6. WARS   ⑧ MADE DRAWINGS OF COPICK+FRITZ + HAIR+YABOO
7. WEAPONS.   WITH MARC PROZZO.

Ⓐ. SENT A DRAWING OF A GUN TO J. EDGAR HOOVER IN 3ᴿᴰ Grd.
(NO REPLY)   THIRD GRADE

TAUGHT SECOND GRADERS WHEN I WAS IN
THE FOURTH GRADE. (CARS MADE OF PAPER CLIPS
(MASKING TAPE +
FASTENERS.

SCHOOLING: SOME ˄LIFE DRAWING IN NINTH GRADE.
ACADEMIC   (WAS THE ONLY CHILD THAT FAILED)

EARLY MUSIC INFLUENCES: WEST SIDE STORY
THE "WATUSI"
ROUND 'BOUT MIDNIGHT
WALKING HAPPY
BLACK ORPHEUS.

CHRONOLOGY

This chronology is mainly excerpted from the 2014 chronology by Franklin Sirmans, among other sources.

1960

December 22: Jean-Michel Basquiat is born at Brooklyn Hospital in Brooklyn, New York. His parents, Gerard Basquiat, born in Port-au-Prince, Haiti, and Matilde Andrades, born in Brooklyn to Puerto Rican parents, live in Park Slope, Brooklyn.

1963

Basquiat's sister Lisane is born in Brooklyn.

1965

Basquiat attends kindergarten in the Head Start program. In these years, he often visits the Brooklyn Museum, the Museum of Modern Art, and the Metropolitan Museum of Art with Matilde, who encourages his interest in art and emphasizes the importance of education.

1966

Basquiat's sister Jeanine is born.

The family moves to East Thirty-Fifth Street in East
Flatbush, Brooklyn.

1967

Basquiat attends Saint Ann's, a progressive private school
in Brooklyn. He becomes an avid reader in Spanish,
French, and English, and a more than competent
athlete, competing in track events.

1968

Basquiat makes cartoon-like drawings inspired by Alfred
Hitchcock films, automobiles, comic books, and the
Alfred E. Neuman character from *Mad* magazine.

May 1968: He is hit by an automobile while playing in
the street. He breaks an arm, suffers various internal
injuries, and has his spleen removed. While recov-
ering, he receives a copy of *Gray's Anatomy* from his
mother. The book makes a lasting impression; its
influence is seen in his later work and in the name
of the band he cofounds in 1979, Gray.

The Basquiats separate and Gerard assumes custody of the three children.

1971

Gerard and the children move to a brownstone in Boerum Hill, Brooklyn. Basquiat leaves Saint Ann's for P.S. 181.

1977

Basquiat creates the fictional character SAMO© (Same Old Shit), who makes a living peddling a fake religion. He begins collaborating with Al Diaz on the SAMO© project.

1978

Basquiat leaves home for good; Gerard gives him some money with the understanding that he will try his best to succeed. He stays with friends, often at the Canal Street loft of British artist/entrepreneur Stan Peskett, where he befriends Fred "Fab 5 Freddy" Brathwaite. Around this time, he also meets Michael

Holman, a future member of the band Gray, and Danny Rosen, and begins frequenting nightclubs. Basquiat, Holman, Rosen, and Vincent Gallo, who would also join Gray, are known as the "baby crowd" in the downtown club scene.

He sells hand-painted postcards and T-shirts to make money. He approaches Andy Warhol and the important curator and critic Henry Geldzahler (who had been appointed Commissioner of Cultural Affairs for New York City in 1977) inside the SoHo restaurant WPA; he sells a postcard to Warhol, but Geldzahler dismisses him as "too young" to be a serious artist.

He becomes a regular in a crowd of filmmakers, musicians, and artists who hang out at the "new" downtown spots: Club 57, CBGB, Hurrah, Tier 3, and, especially, the Mudd Club, where he rubs shoulders with David Byrne, Deborah Harry of Blondie, Madonna, the members of the B-52s, John Laurie, Diego Cortez, Edit DeAk, Ann Magnuson, John Sex, and Patti Astor, cofounder of the Fun Gallery.

Through Brathwaite, he becomes familiar with the new culture flowering uptown in the streets of Harlem

and the basements of the South Bronx: deejaying,
emceeing, creating graffiti, and break dancing—the
formative/primordial elements of hip-hop. Brathwaite notes that "the scene downtown ... was pretty
much all white except for me, Jean-Michel, and a
few other people." Brathwaite introduces Basquiat
to uptown graffitists and rap artists, including Lee
Quiñones, Toxic, A-One, and Rammellzee, a graffiti
artist and deejay with whom Basquiat soon forms a
confrontational, though valuable, friendship.

1979

Basquiat falls out with Diaz shortly after the *Village Voice*
article comes out, ending SAMO© collaboration.
"SAMO© is dead" begins appearing on various SoHo
walls.

He concentrates on painting T-shirts and making postcards, drawings, and collages that combine graffiti art
and abstract expressionism. He collaborates on many
of these works with Jennifer Stein and John Sex and
sells them in Washington Square Park, around SoHo,
and in front of the Museum of Modern Art.

He meets fellow artists and downtown scene makers Keith Haring and Kenny Scharf while wandering around the School of Visual Arts on East Twenty-Third Street. He admires the raw, graffiti-like qualities of Haring's work and sees him as truly belonging to the graffiti subculture in a way that he, Basquiat, does not. The two are close friends for the rest of their lives.

Through Fred Brathwaite, he meets Glenn O'Brien, the producer and host of *TV Party* on New York cable television and a writer for *Interview* magazine. They become good friends, and Basquiat appears frequently on *TV Party*.

Diego Cortez, an artist and filmmaker, sells some of Basquiat's drawings and eventually shows his work to art dealers; he also formally introduces Basquiat to Henry Geldzahler, who becomes a friend and early collector of Basquiat's work.

1980

June: Basquiat participates in *Times Square Show*, his first group exhibition. Held in a vacant building in Times

Square, the show is organized by Colab (Collaborative Projects Incorporated), an artist-run organization based on the Lower East Side, and Fashion Moda,
a graffiti-based alternative gallery space in the South
Bronx. Among the more than one hundred artists in
the show are David Hammons, Jenny Holzer, John
Ahearn, Jane Dickson, Joe Lewis, Lee Quiñones,
Kenny Scharf, and Kiki Smith. *Times Square Show* is
enthusiastically received, an early step in legitimizing
the artists of the East Village club scene and the beginning of a warm, though short-lived, reception
for the graffitists in the New York art world.

1981

February: Basquiat is included in *New York/New Wave*,
a group exhibition organized by Diego Cortez for
P.S.1/Institute for Art and Urban Resources, in Long
Island City, Queens. The show includes more than
twenty artists, including Keith Haring, Robert
Mapplethorpe, Kenny Scharf, Dondi, and Fab 5
Freddy (Brathwaite). Basquiat's work attracts the
attention of dealers Emilio Mazzoli, Bruno
Bischofberger, and Annina Nosei.

April: Brathwaite and Futura organize *Beyond Words: Graffiti-Based-Rooted-Inspired Works* at the Mudd Club. The show includes work by Basquiat (as SAMO©), Keith Haring, Tseng Kwong Chi, Daze, Phase 2, Iggy Pop, Kenny Scharf, and Rammellzee.

May: Basquiat travels to Europe for the first time, for his first solo exhibition at Galleria d'Arte Emilio Mazzoli in Modena, Italy.

September: Annina Nosei invites Basquiat to use her gallery's basement as a studio.

October: He participates in *Public Address*, a group show at Annina Nosei Gallery, New York. Sociopolitical content is the focus of the exhibition, with works by Keith Haring, Jenny Holzer, and Barbara Kruger.

December: The first extensive article on Basquiat, "The Radiant Child," by René Ricard, appears in *Artforum*. The detailed essay examines the emerging New York artists in *Times Square Show*, *New York/New Wave*, and the Mudd Club shows.

1982

March: Basquiat's first solo exhibition in the United
States is held at Annina Nosei Gallery, New York.
Paintings shown include *Arroz con Pollo*, *Self-Portrait*,
Crowns (Peso Neto), and *Untitled (Per Capita)*.

April: He travels to Los Angeles for a solo show at the
Gagosian Gallery. Paintings shown include *Six Crimes*,
Untitled (LA Painting), and *Untitled (Yellow Tar and
Feathers)*.

September: His first solo exhibition at Galerie Bruno
Bischofberger opens in Zürich; it includes the first
showing of his exposed-corner-crossbar paintings.
Works shown include *Man from Naples*, *Crown Hotel*,
and *Multiflavor*.

November: Solo exhibition of his works is held at the
Fun Gallery, located at 254 East Tenth Street and run
by Bill Stelling and Patti Astor. Crowded, "messy"
installation, designed by Basquiat, may have been his
response to criticism that, with rising international
fame and shows in more established SoHo galleries,
his work had lost some of its originality. Paintings
shown include *Cabeza*, *Charles the First*, *Jawbone of an*

Ass, Three Quarters of Olympia Minus the Servant, and *Untitled (Sugar Ray Robinson),* which were among his favorites and which he kept for his personal collection.

1983

March: Basquiat returns to Los Angeles for a second solo show at Gagosian Gallery. Paintings shown include *Jack Johnson, Eyes and Eggs, Hollywood Africans, All Colored Cast (Parts I and II),* and other works featuring images and text related to famous boxers, musicians, and Hollywood films, and the roles black people played in them. Rammellzee and Toxic join him in Los Angeles before the show, and *Hollywood Africans*—now in the collection of the Whitney Museum of American Art—is a portrait of the three friends, their heads floating in a triumvirate over a yellow background.

At age twenty-two, he becomes one of the youngest artists ever to be included in a Whitney Biennial. The exhibition included *Dutch Settlers* and *Untitled (Skull)* and work by more than forty other artists, including Keith Haring, Barbara Kruger, David Salle, and Cindy Sherman.

1984

January: Basquiat's first visit to Maui, Hawaii. He rents a house in the town of Hana, on a remote part of the island, where he sets up a studio to make drawings and paintings with materials sent from Los Angeles.

Boone and Bischofberger become Basquiat's primary dealers, jointly organizing exhibitions.

February: Bischofberger suggests the idea of collaborating with Basquiat to Andy Warhol and Francesco Clemente. Both accept and soon start working with him.

May: His first solo exhibition at Mary Boone Gallery, New York, is a resounding success. Paintings shown include *Bird as Buddha*, *Brown Spots*, *Eye*, *Untitled (Africa)*, and *Wine of Babylon*.

August: His first museum exhibition opens at the Fruitmarket Gallery, Edinburgh, organized by Mark Francis. The exhibition surveys paintings from 1981 to 1984 and travels to the Institute for Contemporary Arts, London, and Boymans van Beuningen Museum, Rotterdam, into 1985.

September: *Collaborations—Basquiat, Clemente, Warhol*, a

group of fifteen paintings, opens at Galerie Bruno
Bischofberger in Zürich.

1985

January: Basquiat's solo exhibition opens at Galerie
   Bruno Bischofberger in Zürich. Paintings shown
   include *Max Roach*, *P-Z*, *Tabac*, and *Zydeco*.
February: He appears on the cover of the *New York Times
   Magazine*, posing barefoot for Cathleen McGuigan's
   extensive article "New Art, New Money: The Market-
   ing of an American Artist."
March: His second solo show opens at Mary Boone
   Gallery, New York. The catalog includes an essay
   by eminent scholar Robert Farris Thompson, who
   situates Basquiat's art in the Afro-Atlantic tradition, a
   context in which it has never before been discussed.
   Paintings shown include *Gold Griot*, *Grillo*, *Flexible*,
   Wicker, and *His Glue-Sniffing Valet*.
September: Sixteen collaborative paintings by Basquiat
   and Warhol are shown at Tony Shafrazi Gallery, New
   York. At Shafrazi's suggestion, the two artists pose together in boxing trunks and gloves for a poster ad-
   vertising the show.

1986

August: Basquiat travels to Africa for the first time, accompanied by his girlfriend, Jennifer Goode, and her brother, Eric. He is joined there by Bruno Bischofberger, who, at Basquiat's urging, arranged for a show in Abidjan, Côte d'Ivoire. Paintings shown include *Charles the First* and *Jawbone of an Ass*.

November: A large survey exhibition of more than sixty paintings and drawings, organized by Carl Haenlien, opens at the Kestnergesellschaft in Hannover. At age twenty-five, Basquiat is the youngest artist ever to be given an exhibition there.

1987

February 22: Andy Warhol dies at age fifty-eight after gallbladder surgery at New York Hospital. Although the friendship had suffered in the past year as their work had moved in different directions, Basquiat is devastated and paints *Gravestone* in memoriam, then becomes more reclusive, often refusing to see friends.

1988

January: Vrej Baghoomian arranges for an exhibition of Basquiat's new paintings for just one night in the Cable Building, SoHo, before they are sent to shows in Paris and Düsseldorf.

Basquiat travels to Paris for a solo show at Galerie Yvon Lambert. Paintings shown include *Light Blue Movers*, *Riddle Me This Batman*, and *She Installs Confidence and Picks His Brain Like a Salad*. Later in January, he travels to Düsseldorf for a solo exhibition at the Galerie Hans Mayer.

April: He travels to New Orleans with Ouattara Watts for Jazz Fest.

June: He spends time in Maui and returns to New York at the end of the month, having stopped for a week in Los Angeles.

August 12: Jean-Michel Basquiat dies in his Great Jones Street loft at age twenty-seven.

August 17: A private funeral is held at Frank E. Campbell Funeral Chapel, Madison Avenue and Eighty-First Street. The funeral is attended by immediate family and close friends, including Keith Haring, Francesco

Clemente, and Paige Powell. Jeffrey Deitch delivers the eulogy. Basquiat is buried at Greenwood Cemetery in Brooklyn.

November 5: About three hundred friends and admirers attend a memorial gathering at Saint Peter's Church, Lexington Avenue and Fifty-Fourth Street. Music is played by surviving members of Gray and others; Fred Brathwaite recites Langston Hughes's "Genius Child" (1937), and Suzanne Mallouk delivers a particularly moving reading of A. R. Penck's "Poem for Basquiat" (1984).

1990

February 16: Keith Haring dies of AIDS at age thirty-one.

November: Robert Miller Gallery, New York, and the Estate of Jean-Michel Basquiat present a survey of Basquiat's drawings, along with an accompanying catalog.

December 15: A memorial exhibition of Keith Haring's and Basquiat's work opens at Tony Shafrazi Gallery, New York.

1992

October: The Whitney Museum of American Art, New York, presents the first major retrospective exhibition, *Jean-Michel Basquiat*, curated by Richard Marshall.

1994

Exhibitions of Basquiat's works are held at Henry Art Gallery, Seattle; Galerie Delta, Rotterdam; and Robert Miller Gallery, New York. Another exhibition, *Jean-Michel Basquiat: The Blue Ribbon Series*, travels from Mount Holyoke College Art Museum in South Hadley, Massachusetts, to the Wadsworth Atheneum, Hartford, Connecticut; Andy Warhol Museum, Pittsburgh; and Neuberger Museum of Art, Purchase, New York, into 1996.

1996

Solo exhibitions of Basquiat's works are held at the Serpentine Gallery, London, and Palacio Episcopal de Málaga. Enrico Navarra publishes a two-volume book on Basquiat's paintings.

August: The film *Basquiat*, directed by Julian Schnabel and featuring Jeffrey Wright, David Bowie, Dennis Hopper, and Gary Oldman, is released by Miramax Films.

1997
Basquiat's works are presented at the Kaohsiung Museum of Fine Arts, Kaohsiung, China; Taichung Museum, Taiwan; Fondation Dina Vierny-Musée Maillol, Paris; Gallery Hyundai, Seoul; Mitsukoshi Museum, Tokyo; and Museo Nacional de Bellas Artes, Buenos Aires.

1998
Solo exhibitions of Basquiat's works are held at the Museu de Arte Moderna, Recife, Brazil, and the Pinacoteca, São Paulo.

1999
February–May: Large exhibitions of Basquiat's works are held at the KunstHausWien, Vienna, accompanied by a catalog.

June: The survey exhibition *Basquiat a Venezia* opens at Fondazione Bevilacqua La Masa as part of the Venice Biennale.

October: The exhibition *Jean-Michel Basquiat: Selected Paintings and Drawings* opens at Tony Shafrazi Gallery, New York, with a book published by Shafrazi on the artist's paintings and a book on his drawings published by Galerie Enrico Navarra.

2000

November: *Basquiat en La Habana* is presented as part of the Seventh Biennial de La Habana, accompanied by a catalog.

2002

Exhibitions of Basquiat's works are shown at Gagosian Gallery, Beverly Hills (of collaborative paintings with Warhol), and Galerie Sho, Tokyo. *Jean-Michel Basquiat: War Paint*, at Spike Gallery, New York, is accompanied by a catalog with an essay by Libby Lumpkin.

2004

Basquiat's works are included in the exhibition *Latin American and Caribbean Art: MoMA at El Museo*, organized jointly by the Museum of Modern Art and El Museo del Barrio, New York.

2005

March: The Brooklyn Museum—where Basquiat spent formative years looking at art—opens an exhibition of more than one hundred paintings and drawings. This second major retrospective travels to the Museum of Contemporary Art, Los Angeles, and the Museum of Fine Arts, Houston, through February 2006.

2006

May: *Jean-Michel Basquiat: 1981, The Studio of the Street*, curated by Diego Cortez and Glenn O'Brien, opens at Deitch Projects, New York, accompanied by a catalog.

2008

December: Basquiat's works are included in *30 Americans*, an exhibition of works by African American artists at the Rubell Family Collection, Miami.

2009

December: *Jean-Michel Basquiat: The Radiant Child*, directed by Tamra Davis and produced by Arthouse Films, is previewed at Art Basel, Miami Beach.

2010

January: The final cut of *Jean-Michel Basquiat: The Radiant Child* premieres at the Sundance Film Festival.

May: A major retrospective curated by Dieter Buchhart and Sam Keller opens at the Fondation Beyeler, Basel, in the year Basquiat would have turned fifty. In October, the exhibition travels to the Musée d'Art Moderne de la Ville de Paris.

2012–14

Basquiat's work is included in many major museum and traveling group exhibitions, including *Blues for Smoke* at the Museum of Contemporary Art, Los Angeles, which later travels to the Whitney Museum of American Art, New York, and Wexner Center for the Arts, Columbus; and *Caribbean: Crosswords of the World*, held at El Museo del Barrio, the Queens Museum, and the Studio Museum in Harlem, New York.

2013

February–April: A retrospective exhibition of Basquiat's work is held at the Gagosian Gallery, West Twenty-Fourth Street, New York.

May–June: Sotheby's (New York) holds *Man Made: Jean-Michel Basquiat*, an exhibition of more than thirty of Basquiat's works, most of which have rarely or never been seen in public and are offered for sale.

May–August: The Gagosian Gallery, Hong Kong, shows a smaller exhibition of Basquiat's work and uncharacteristically shifts focus to his later works.

2014

May–June: *Jean-Michel Basquiat Drawing: Works from the Schorr Family Collection* is held at Acquavella Galleries, New York, featuring works from the collection of Herbert and Lenore Schorr, who were friends of Basquiat's and began collecting his works in 1981.

October: *Basquiat and the Bayou* opens at the Ogden Museum of Southern Art, New Orleans.

2015

April: *Basquiat: The Unknown Notebooks* opens at the Brooklyn Museum in April. Never before exhibited in full, Basquiat's notebooks provide unique insight into the artist's creative process and the importance of language and the written word in his aesthetic. A facsimile of the notebooks has been published by Princeton University Press.

February: *Now's the Time* opens at the Art Gallery of Ontario, Toronto, and travels to the Guggenheim Bilbao.

2016

May: *Words Are All We Have* opens at Nahmad Contemporary, New York.

2016–17

Basquiat: The Unknown Notebooks travels to the High Museum of Art, Atlanta; the Pérez Art Museum, Miami; and the Cleveland Museum of Art, Cleveland.

2017

February: *Basquiat before Basquiat: East 12th Street, 1979–1980* opens at the Museum of Contemporary Art, Denver, Colorado, and travels to the Cranbrook Art Museum, Bloomfield Hills, Michigan.

May: *Untitled (1982)* sells for a record $110.5 million at Sotheby's, becoming the sixth most expensive work ever sold at auction.

September: *Boom for Real* opens at the Barbican Art Gallery, London, and travels to the Schirn Kunsthalle, Frankfurt am Main.

2018

January: *One Basquiat*, the first museum presentation of
  Untitled (1982), opens at the Brooklyn Museum.
October: *Jean-Michel Basquiat—Egon Schiele* opens at the
  Fondation Louis Vuitton, Paris. A French translation
  of *The Notebooks* is published by Princeton University
  Press in conjunction with the show.

2019

Major exhibitions of Basquiat's work are scheduled
  to open at the Brandt Foundation, New York; the
  National Gallery of Victoria, Melbourne; the
  Guggenheim Museum, New York; and the Mori
  Art Museum, Tokyo.

ACKNOWLEDGMENTS

The words on these pages belong solely to Jean-Michel Basquiat, and it is to him I owe my greatest thanks, yet this book is a result of the hard work and dedication of many amazing individuals.

I cannot overstate my gratitude for the continued support and encouragement of Jeanine, Lisane, and the entire Basquiat family throughout the years. Their work expands upon the incredible energy of Gerard Basquiat and his tireless promotion of Jean-Michel's legacy during his lifetime. His spirit and force has been an inspiration to me and many others. Many thanks as well to Nora Fitzpatrick. It remains an honor and a privilege to be aligned with this incredible family and legacy.

Thank you to David Stark for his special contributions and to him and his team for their incredible accomplishments in bringing Jean-Michel's work to a worldwide audience.

My thanks as well to Henry Geldzahler, who exposed me early on to Jean-Michel's work. René Ricard was also crucial in shaping my journey with Jean-Michel's work, most notably as the catalyst for my purchase of the "unknown notebooks."

I am immensely grateful to Carlo McCormick for his invaluable insights, guidance, and active participation throughout the formation of this book.

My heartfelt appreciation to Michelle Komie, Pamela Weidman, Terri O'Prey, Cathy Slovensky, Julia Haav, Erin Suydam, and everyone at Princeton University Press for their continued professionalism, encouragement, and passion for our projects together throughout the years, and a special thank you to Mitchell Julis.

Special thanks to Franklin Sirmans for allowing us to draw from his exceptional chronology and for his long years of friendship, and to Lotte Johnson for her additional work developing the chronology. Special thanks as well to Anke Wiedmann for her outstanding research and support of this publication, and to Dieter Buchhart for his years of collaboration and support. Thanks as well to Anna Hofbauer for her guidance.

Additional thanks to: Rich Colicchio, Mary-Ann Monforton, Lee Jaffe, Hannah Alderfer, Jeffrey Deitch, Janet and Jonathan Geldzahler, Julia Gruen, Hiroko Onoda, Tony Shafrazi,

Patti Astor, Bill Stelling, Stephen Lack, Eleanor Nairne, Nick Taylor, Michael Holman, Enrico Navarra, Géraldine Levy, Ted Beckstead, Sara Citarella, Alex DeRonde, Fab 5 Freddy, Futura, Lou Sager, Mike Dean, Louise Donegan, Derek Ali, Sickamore, Carlos W Desrosiers, John Pelosi, and John Cahill.

In memoriam: Kiely Jenkins, Keith Haring, Allan Arnold, Bobby Breslau, Arch Connelly, Michael Stewart, Tseng Kwong Chi, David Wojnarowicz, Adolfo Sanchez, Dan Friedman, John Sex, Rammellzee, Christine Zounek, and O.W.

Special thanks to Fiona Graham for her invaluable research and organization. Thanks to Taliesin Thomas for her amazing editorial assistance, and Steven Rodríguez, Bill Eagen, Zara Hoffman, and Amanda Scoledes for their continued support.

My sincere gratitude as well to Ai Weiwei for his years of friendship and continued inspiration.

Finally, I give all my thanks to my amazing wife, Abbey, and my wonderful children, Justin, Ethan, Ellie, and Jonah, for their love and encouragement. And as always, my love and thanks to my mother, Judith.

LARRY WARSH
NEW YORK CITY
MARCH 2019

ILLUSTRATIONS